HALLOWEEN IDEAS

WRITTEN BY
JULIA MARCH AND SELINA WOOD

MODELS BY
ALICE FINCH AND JASON BRISCOE

CONTENTS

HAVE A SPOOKTACULAR HALLOWEEN, EVERYONE!

WITCH'S CATS

A lonely witch could get up to all kinds of mischief, so build some feline friends to keep her company. You won't need a litter box for these magnificent kitties—just a box of bricks!

THERE'S ROOM ON MY BROOM FOR ONE MORE!

TOP TIP
A black cat is said to bring good luck only if it is facing toward you. Build one with a face on each side, just to be sure!

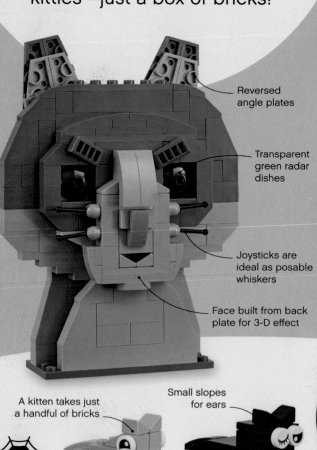

Reversed angle plates

Transparent green radar dishes

Joysticks are ideal as posable whiskers

Face built from back plate for 3-D effect

Staring eye tiles

Single stud makes a cute cat nose

Try a red collar and tail tip!

A kitten takes just a handful of bricks

Small slopes for ears

GHOSTLY DOORS

Knock knock! A ghost doesn't have to open the door to find out who's there. It just pokes its face through! Make some spooky-eyed doors to give trick-or-treaters a chilling unwelcome.

WHOOO'S KNOCKING?!

Life preserver as door knocker

Plates with studs

Build a brick wall to set your door into

MAIL A LETTER ... I DARE YOU!

Is this a ghost pretending to be a minifigure?

DID THAT DOOR JUST TALK?

9

TRICK-OR-TREAT HOUSES

Build some house fronts to attract passing trick-or-treaters. Don't forget the creepy decorations! You could add a guard spider on the roof to welcome visitors—or to warn them off.

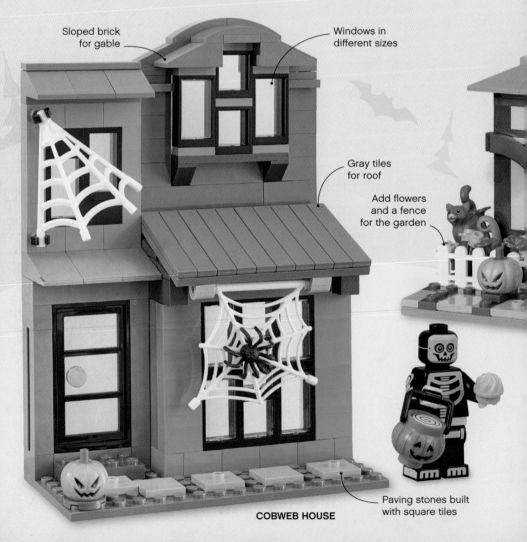

Sloped brick for gable

Windows in different sizes

Gray tiles for roof

Add flowers and a fence for the garden

Paving stones built with square tiles

COBWEB HOUSE

2x2 hinge brick

TOP TIP
You don't have to build a house from scratch. You can use an existing LEGO® house and make it spooky!

Row of sloped bricks for roof

Round corner bricks make spider's body

Large leaf on pumpkin

PUMPKIN HOUSE

Pumpkins invite trick-or-treaters

BRICK OR TREAT?

11

GHOULISH YARD

Create a bone-chilling graveyard scene complete with scary skeletons. Dig into your store of LEGO® bricks and build a creepy cart, ghoulish gates, and a bat-topped gravestone.

Tall bricks with side clips as gateposts

GHOULISH GATES

BAT-TOPPED GRAVESTONE

Cart decorated with bones

Hinge plate allows cart to tip up

Flames pieces

I'M READY FOR THE NIGHT SHIFT!

Round tile attaches to connector piece

Spoked cart wheels

CREEPY CART

13

VEGGIE-LOVING VAMPIRES

Vampires love Halloween—it's the perfect night for a bite. Why not bring some vampires to life to enjoy their favorite feast? These two use their fangs to chomp on fruit and vegetables!

Black curved brick for dark hair

I'M A SUCKER FOR HALLOWEEN!

Wings clip into stud brick

FAMILY PET BAT

Spider could be a pet or a hair clip

Cobweb forms lace collar

Red curved slopes form a cape

VAMPIRE GIRL

Arches add flare to cloak

MR. VAMPIRE

CURIOUS BUCKETS

Every trick-or-treater needs a Halloween bucket! Make some creepy containers to store your treats in. They aren't tricky to make and they're sure to keep your treats safe.

TOP TIP

Search your LEGO collection for handy bricks you can use for eyes, noses, and other facial features. Even banana pieces will work!

Bendy hoses or tubes are ideal handles

Flat plates create front and back of bucket

Black stud for wart

Segmented leg piece for mouth

THEY'RE HANDY FOR CANDY!

SPOT THE DIFFERENCE

Here's a tricky Halloween-themed puzzle to challenge your friends. They will have to be as sharp-eyed as an owl to find all eight differences between these two spooky scenes.

Shield piece with tile for ancient door decoration

Binoculars look like hinges

WHAT'S CHANGED?

There are a few ways to create differences between your models. You could swap one part for another, change a color, move things around, or add or remove pieces. The sneakier, the better!

Answers to the puzzle below are on page 76

HOW TO PLAY

1 Build two identical models, then change a few details on one of them. Six to ten changes is a good number.

2 Tell a friend how many differences there are to look for. Then challenge them to spot every one.

3 Play as many times as you like, changing the differences each time.

Cobweb held in place with clips

Use red leaf pieces for a spooky tree

Plant stems next to gravestone

SPOOKY FOREST

Who would dare take a walk in this freaky forest? Build a weird, wild wood filled with spooky plants and trees with eyes. What was that noise? A bird, a deer, or something supernatural?

Spider lurks on tree branch

Plant leaves

LEGO® Technic angle connectors form a crooked trunk

TRY THIS
For a fantasy feel, instead of green or brown leaves try poisonous pinks or bizarre blues!

DID SOMEONE SAY "SPOOKY"?

Build up layers of leaves on plates

1x3 plate

Hanging vines ready to grab passersby

Forest ogre in a haunted stump

Spiky plant stalks on small cones

19

GHOST-TRAPPER

Pesky poltergeists come out to play at Halloween!
Build this clever ghost-trapper to suck them up
out of mischief. There's enough room inside for
a whole host of ghouls and ghosts!

Ribbed hose
transfers ghost
to canister

Handle of
control panel

Radar dish
sucks up ghost

Speaker shrieks when
ghost is caught

Angled plates as owl ears

I'LL KEEP WATCH FROM UP HIGH

Face wings inward for roosting pose

OWL

FUNNY FAMILIARS

Familiars are animal helpers who work for witches or wizards. Why not make some quirky creatures of your own? Try a big-eyed owl to watch over you or a sneaky mouse spy.

I'LL LOOK OUT DOWN BELOW

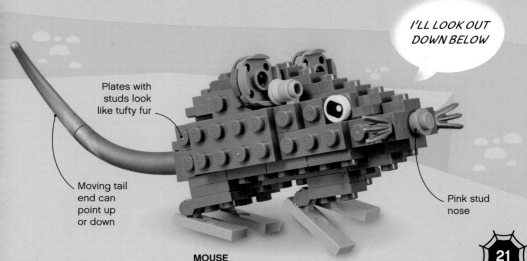

Plates with studs look like tufty fur

Moving tail end can point up or down

Pink stud nose

MOUSE

GIANT
SPIDER

Trick your friends and family with this supersized, spooky spider. Its eight legs can even move up and down—what a creepy crawly!

Legs can move up or down to make creepy poses

SPECIAL BRICK

This curved, segmented piece is just right for a spider's leg. You can also use it as a tail or a rib.

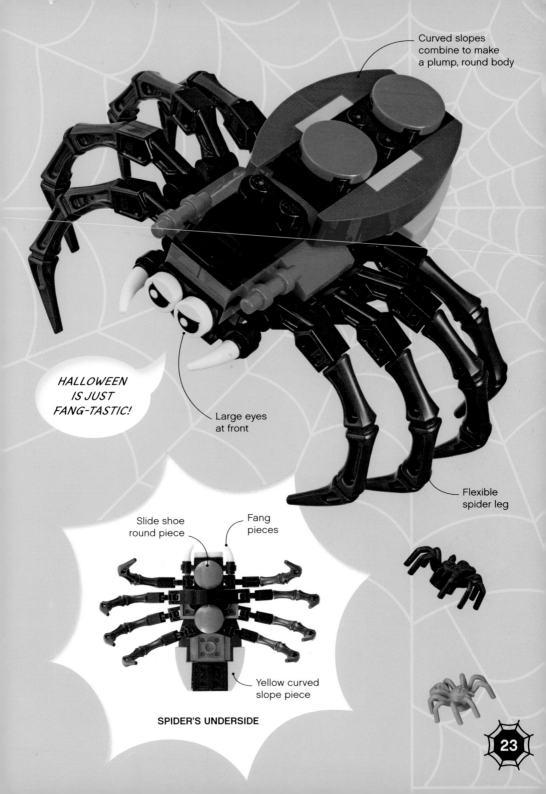

Curved slopes
combine to make
a plump, round body

HALLOWEEN
IS JUST
FANG-TASTIC!

Large eyes
at front

Flexible
spider leg

Slide shoe
round piece

Fang
pieces

Yellow curved
slope piece

SPIDER'S UNDERSIDE

23

MONSTER MIX

Create a monster mash-up! Build some Halloween heroes, such as a witch, a werewolf, and a pumpkin man. Then swap their body parts around at random until you have a medley of mixed-up monsters.

LEGO Technic axle

LEGO Technic connector peg

Pumpkin man's body

Witch's hat made from black cone pieces

PUMPKIN MAN

Ears are 1x1 plate bars

Clip tile for werewolf claws

WEREWOLF

WITCH

HOW TO PLAY

1 With your friends, build some Halloween creatures with separate head, body, and leg parts.

2 Take the creatures apart and place all the pieces into three different piles for heads, bodies, and legs.

3 Take turns to close your eyes and take a piece from each pile.

4 Build a mash-up monster with the head, body, and leg pieces you have picked. Whose monster is the craziest?

Witch's hat and head

Pumpkin man's head

Witch's legs

PUMPY WITCHKIN

Werewolf's legs

WITCHWOLF

Witch's body

Pumpkin man's legs

WACKY WEREWITCH

ARGH! WHICH WITCH IS WHICH?

25

CREEPY CRAWLIES

It's not just ghouls that sneak around on Halloween night, creepy crawlies love it, too. Make some wacky critters with goggle eyes, spiky legs, and extra-long antennae.

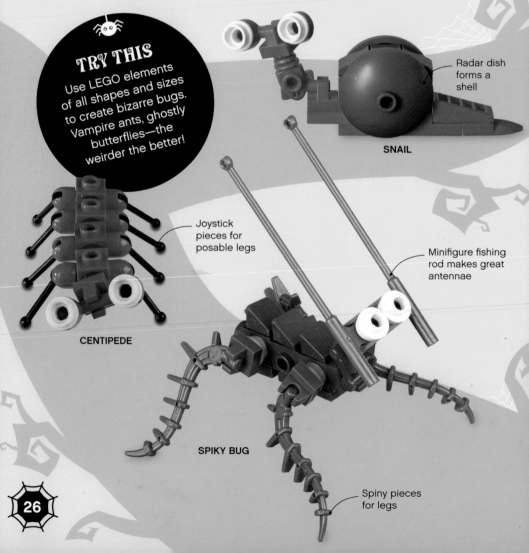

TRY THIS
Use LEGO elements of all shapes and sizes to create bizarre bugs. Vampire ants, ghostly butterflies—the weirder the better!

Radar dish forms a shell

SNAIL

Joystick pieces for posable legs

Minifigure fishing rod makes great antennae

CENTIPEDE

SPIKY BUG

Spiny pieces for legs

HALLOWEEN CANDLES

Create a Halloween atmosphere with some eerie but elegant candles. They won't drip or melt, and they'll never get any shorter—unless you remove some pieces, of course!

Drip shield is a radar dish

NOW I CAN SEE IN THE DARK!

Bright Halloween colors

Large flames suggest a roaring blaze

Bat wings can be flipped up or down

Four black scorpions make a scary base for a candlestick

Wide base for stability

Crossed swords

Row of tooth plates

BACK VIEW

Mast is a stack of round bricks topped with a flagpole

Skull-and-crossbones flag

White robot arms look like knobbly bones

GHOST SHIP

Spooks, ahoy! Keep the Halloween spirit afloat by building a ghostly galleon with a crew of zombie pirates. Don't forget to add a skull-and-crossbones flag, or your pirates might make you walk the plank.

TRY THIS

Get your galleon ready to sail with lanterns, crossed swords at the stern, and ladders for the crew to scamper up. Be creative!

HELP! SKELETON OVERBOARD!

Torn sails made of curved pieces look ready to rattle in the wind

You could add a minifigure head at the prow to bring your ship luck

WACKY WITCH FACE

Team up with your friends to create a wacky witch portrait. Take turns to be blindfolded and add zany LEGO pieces, such as handcuffs and cobwebs, to the witch's face. The results will be frightfully funny!

HOW TO PLAY

1 First, make a blank witch's face out of flat LEGO plates.

2 One by one, put on a blindfold (a scarf is ideal) and add an unusual LEGO piece as an eye, nose, mouth and so on. No peeking!

3 The witch will end up with funny features all over her face!

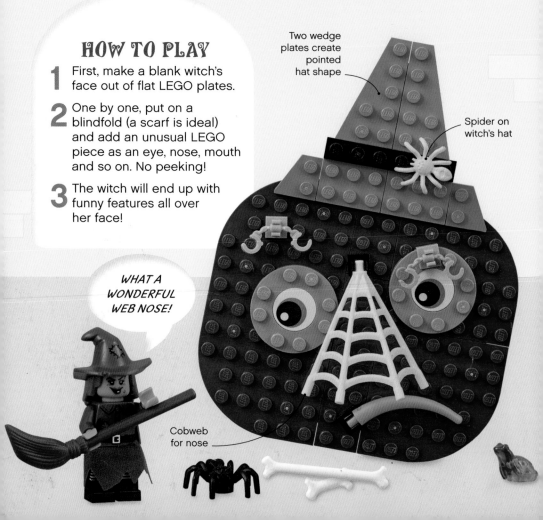

Two wedge plates create pointed hat shape

Spider on witch's hat

WHAT A WONDERFUL WEB NOSE!

Cobweb for nose

GHOST-O-METER

Build this handy ghost-o-meter to help you in your phantom-hunting quest. It will soon tell you when a ghost is close by, even if the sneaky spook has made itself invisible!

THEY'RE ONTO ME! TIME TO FLY ...

Specter detector panels

Skull revealed when meter is on

Antenna swivels on ball joint

Open cover reveals battery

Turning dial is tooth plate on a round tile with one stud

SLIDING PANEL RAISED

13x8 wing

Purple bricks add a dash of color

Two studs look like nostrils

FLYING BAT

Plate with bar is ear

Dragon wing

Tile with pin connects to wing

Bats have great hearing, so give yours big ears

LEGO Technic ball joints make beady bat eyes

TOP TIP
Don't stop building bats if you run out of wings! Experiment and use angled pieces and claws to make wing shapes instead.

Wings and body built in one piece

CUTE BAT

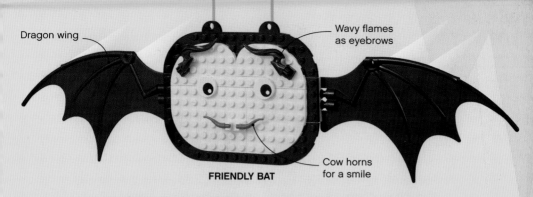

Dragon wing

Wavy flames as eyebrows

FRIENDLY BAT

Cow horns for a smile

GOING BATTY

Create your own bat colony—of flat bats, cute bats, angry bats, and sleepy bats! Build some using plates with holes, so you can hang them up and watch them fly.

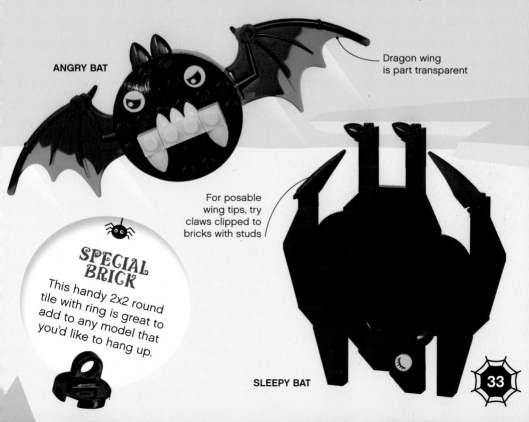

ANGRY BAT

Dragon wing is part transparent

For posable wing tips, try claws clipped to bricks with studs

SPECIAL BRICK

This handy 2x2 round tile with ring is great to add to any model that you'd like to hang up.

SLEEPY BAT

33

DISMAL DUNGEON

Build a deep, dark dungeon for a badly behaved skeleton. Fill it with chains, cobwebs, and scampering rats. Then add a dungeon dinner—mouldy cheese and warm water!

Spiral staircase

Round piece for dungeon dinner table

Rectangular tile lid

Two 1x2 hinge bricks

Green tooth pieces

Webs come in all shapes and sizes

TOP TIP

Why not post a minifigure guard at the top of the stairs to stop any escape attempts? A skeleton knight is a good choice.

I'M THE GHOSTLY GUARD FOR THE JOB!

Chest for storing bones

EERIE EYEBALL

This delicious-looking apple is a juicy sight, until you turn it around. Suddenly it's a big, scary eyeball! Your friends won't be able to stop staring at it—and the eyeball will stare right back.

Use round corner bricks to create curve

Round 1x1 stud on plate for stalk

2x1 curved slope

BACK VIEW

A 1x2 plate with teeth looks like eyelashes

WHAT A SPOOKY SIGHT!

FRONT VIEW

HALLOWEEN DRESS-UP

Halloween is all about the costumes. Build some ghastly props such as bat ears, vampire fangs, and tendril hair. Then get grimacing for some spooky Halloween selfies.

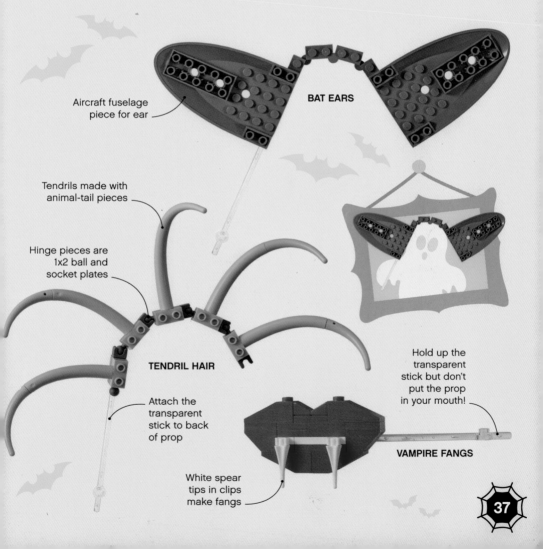

Aircraft fuselage piece for ear

BAT EARS

Tendrils made with animal-tail pieces

Hinge pieces are 1x2 ball and socket plates

TENDRIL HAIR

Attach the transparent stick to back of prop

Hold up the transparent stick but don't put the prop in your mouth!

VAMPIRE FANGS

White spear tips in clips make fangs

BONY DRAGONS

Build some dragon skeletons with fierce jaws, claws, and horns. They may be a bit on the bony side, but when they come to life, your Halloween will really start to rattle!

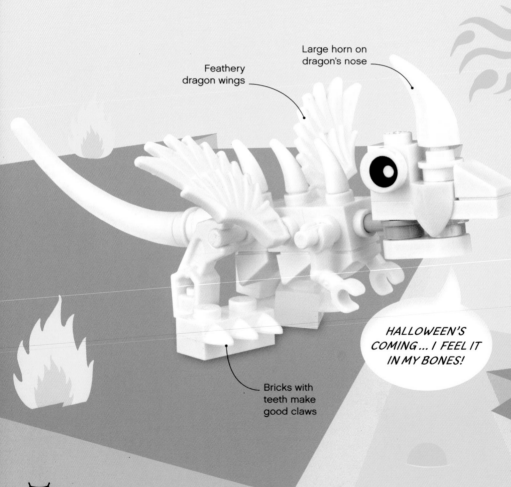

Feathery dragon wings

Large horn on dragon's nose

Bricks with teeth make good claws

HALLOWEEN'S COMING... I FEEL IT IN MY BONES!

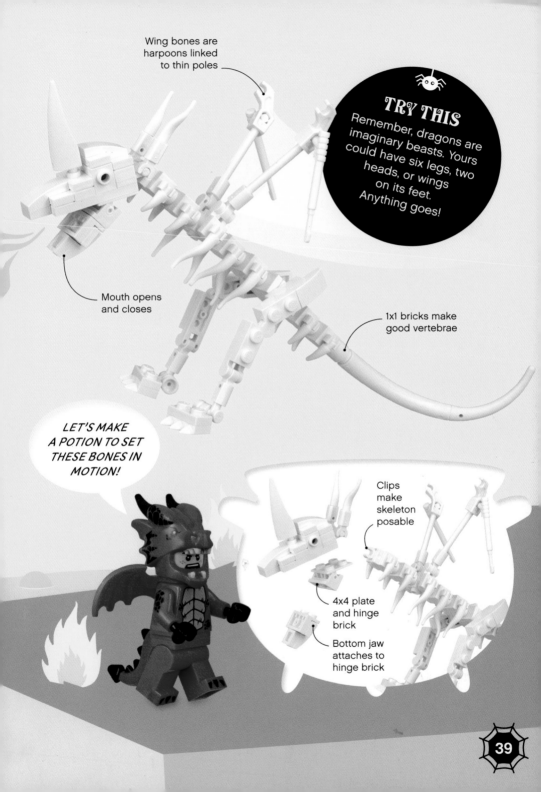

Wing bones are harpoons linked to thin poles

TRY THIS
Remember, dragons are imaginary beasts. Yours could have six legs, two heads, or wings on its feet. Anything goes!

Mouth opens and closes

1x1 bricks make good vertebrae

LET'S MAKE A POTION TO SET THESE BONES IN MOTION!

Clips make skeleton posable

4x4 plate and hinge brick

Bottom jaw attaches to hinge brick

SORCERERS' HOUSES

Build a magical house for a witch or wizard and furnish it in style. Forget sofas and TVs—these sorcerers need potions, spell books, and maybe an herb garden in the yard. Of course, a cauldron in the kitchen is a must!

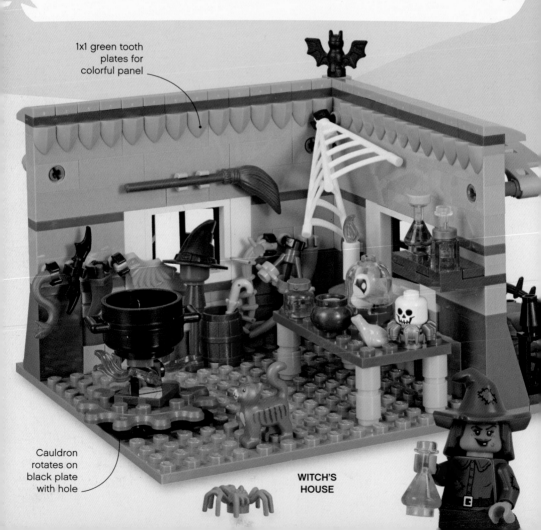

1x1 green tooth plates for colorful panel

Cauldron rotates on black plate with hole

WITCH'S HOUSE

Skeleton piece hangs from brick with side stud

Brown 1x1 brick attached to slope looks like timber beam

WIZARD'S HOUSE

Make flames with transparent orange and yellow bricks

TOP TIP
Decide what you want to hang up in the house before you build the walls. Then build bricks with studs for clips into the walls in the correct places.

JUST ONE MORE RAT HAIR SHOULD DO IT!

Top of owl post has brown twigs

Canopy is made with LEGO® Technic piece

Herb garden with grasses, vines, and toadstools

BACK VIEW OF WITCH'S HOUSE

GAME SET-UP

1 Build a board, then use colorful 2x2 tiles to make winding paths, with several branches, from one side to the opposite side.

2 Set out some scary obstacles along the course. There must be at least one on each branch of the path.

3 Create some game pieces, one for each player.

4 Write down a list of different commands for each obstacle, such as "spider = go back five squares" or "scorpion = take an extra turn."

Cat arch marks the finish

Paths must meet, or players will get stranded

HOW TO PLAY

1 Players take turns to roll a die and move their game piece along the route. If they land on or pass by an obstacle, they must obey the command.

2 The first to reach the end of the course is the winner!

Small LEGO® parts attached to studs make good game pieces

GAME PIECES

BEASTLY BOARD GAME

Build a hair-raising Halloween game to play with your friends. Who will be the first person to get past the obstacles on this creepy course?

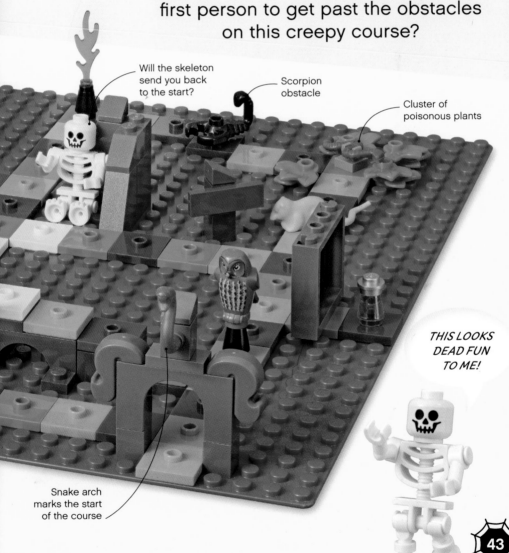

Will the skeleton send you back to the start?

Scorpion obstacle

Cluster of poisonous plants

Snake arch marks the start of the course

THIS LOOKS DEAD FUN TO ME!

DRAGON GUARD

Build a baby dragon to keep the spooks at bay. This big-hearted beast may look cute, but when it breathes out fire, the Halloween ghouls are sure to scatter!

Wing attaches to ball socket so it can move up and down

Curved and sloped bricks make body

WHAT A NIGHT FOR A FLIGHT!

Green pointed piece for a tail

Curved slope with studs

Red flippers for feet

TOP TIP
Why not add some spikes to the dragon's body? A row of 1x1 clips that stick out will be perfect.

White plates form cobwebs

Ghosts attach with 1x1 stud bricks

BEST-DRESSED DECORATIONS

Conjure up some magic for your Halloween party with these delightful decorations. Build flat shapes and bring them to life with ghosts, bats, witches' hats, and spiders' webs.

Feet are the fingers of a 1x2 hinge plate

I JUST CAN'T WAIT TO HAUNT THESE!

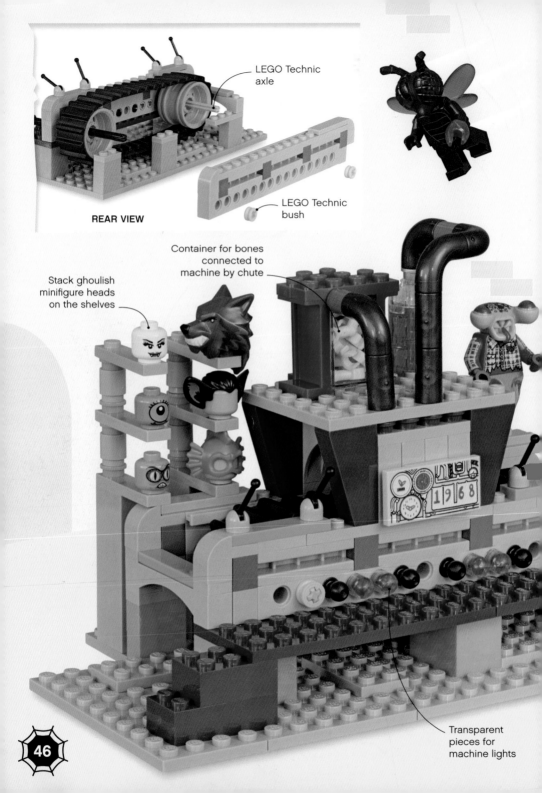

LEGO Technic
axle

LEGO Technic
bush

REAR VIEW

Container for bones
connected to
machine by chute

Stack ghoulish
minifigure heads
on the shelves

Transparent
pieces for
machine lights

MONSTER MACHINE

What mixed-up monster muddle will this machine churn out? Build one of your own and load it with minifigure parts. Then crank up the machine by turning the handle to move the conveyor belt.

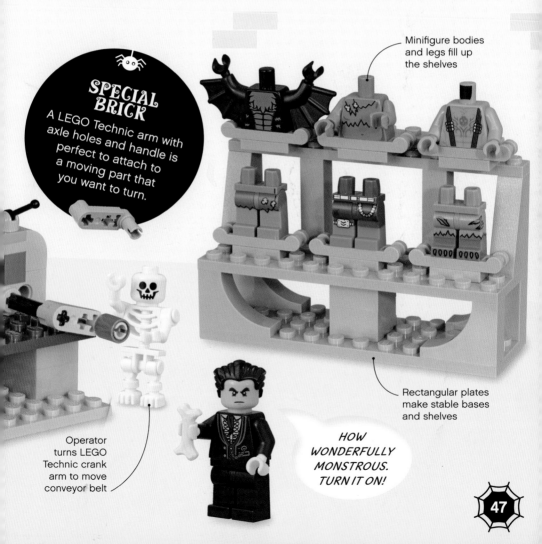

Minifigure bodies and legs fill up the shelves

SPECIAL BRICK
A LEGO Technic arm with axle holes and handle is perfect to attach to a moving part that you want to turn.

Rectangular plates make stable bases and shelves

Operator turns LEGO Technic crank arm to move conveyor belt

HOW WONDERFULLY MONSTROUS. TURN IT ON!

PUMPKIN
GARDEN

Create a garden of ghoulish gourds—it's as easy as pumpkin pie! Pick orange pieces for ripe pumpkins and green for unripe ones. Why not make one pumpkin hollow to hold a little Halloween treat.

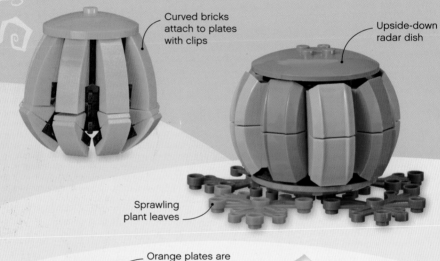

Curved bricks attach to plates with clips

Upside-down radar dish

Sprawling plant leaves

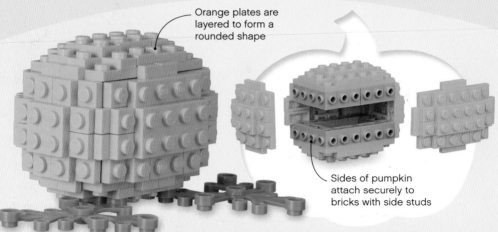

Orange plates are layered to form a rounded shape

Sides of pumpkin attach securely to bricks with side studs

SPOOKY SKULLS

Build some super skull table decorations. Use LEGO® elements of all shapes and colors to make unusual eyes, noses, and mouths. Then your skulls are sure to surprise your party guests!

Build skull shape from curved and rectangular plates

Wave flames look like horns

Leaf pieces with holes for spiky hair

Bat wings

3x2 tiles with holes as lips

READY FOR SOME SKULLDUGGERY?

49

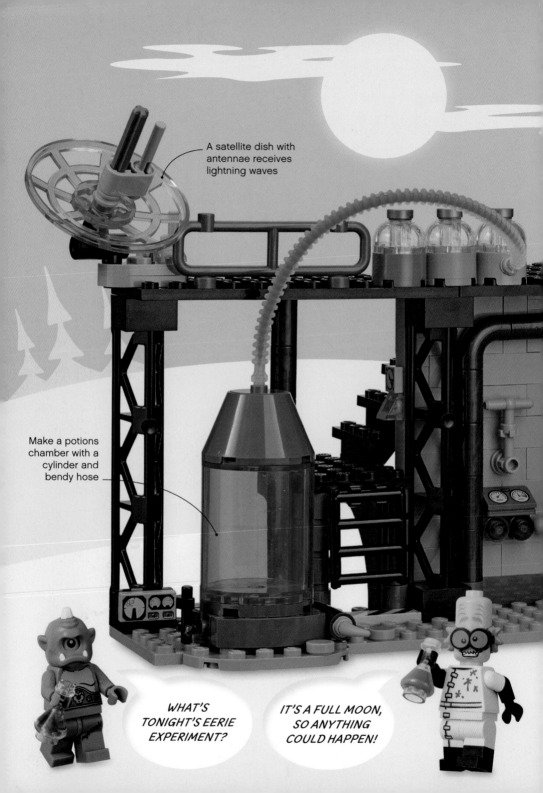

MAD SCIENTIST'S LAB

A mad scientist needs a zany-looking laboratory. Fill your lab with as many gadgets, tubes, and containers as you can. But watch out, the scientist might succeed in bringing some monsters to life!

Add a chair for a minifigure

Multiphoton Optigalvanic Spectroscopy

2nm WV

TRY THIS

Add bricks or minifigure parts to the potion chamber. What do you think the mad scientist is creating?

Stairs up to the viewing platform

Door is hinged to open

BACK VIEW

51

HALLOWEEN
BUILD CHALLENGE

Test your creativity and brush up your building skills with this fun LEGO® challenge. You will need quick fingers and a quick mind to win this Halloween-themed game!

HOW TO PLAY

1 Each player writes five build ideas on pieces of paper.

2 Fold the papers and put them into a bag. Everyone then picks an idea out at random.

3 Set a timer for five minutes, and get building!

4 When the time is up, players try to guess what each build is.

5 A correct guess gets the builder and guesser two points each. The top scorer is the winner.

Claw and radar dish witch's hat

Purple robes for Halloween party dress

WITCH

Transparent round bricks and dome top

POTION BOTTLE

Gather a few handfuls of random bricks

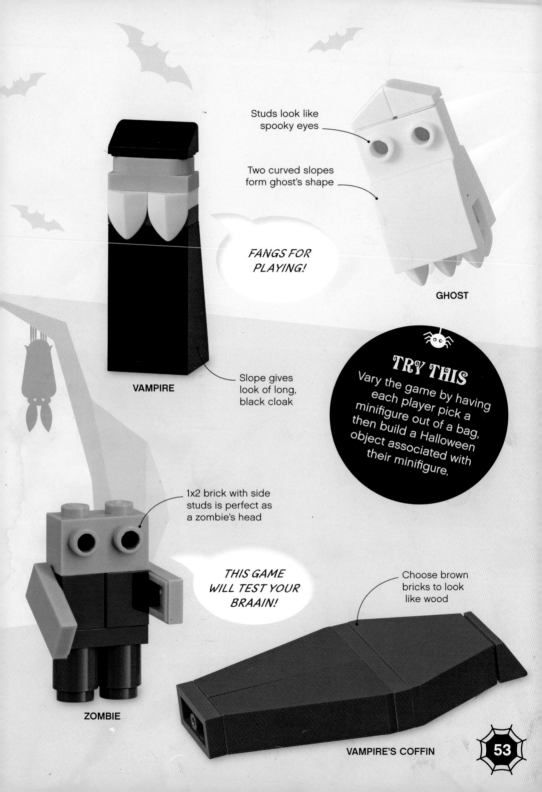

Studs look like
spooky eyes

Two curved slopes
form ghost's shape

GHOST

*FANGS FOR
PLAYING!*

Slope gives
look of long,
black cloak

VAMPIRE

TRY THIS
Vary the game by having
each player pick a
minifigure out of a bag,
then build a Halloween
object associated with
their minifigure.

1x2 brick with side
studs is perfect as
a zombie's head

*THIS GAME
WILL TEST YOUR
BRAAIN!*

Choose brown
bricks to look
like wood

ZOMBIE

VAMPIRE'S COFFIN

GHOST TRAIN

All aboard! This ghost train is picking up passengers for a hair-raising ride past bats, giant spiders, and monsters. What's on the other side of the tracks is anyone's guess. Turn the page to find out ...

WOW, THIS IS FREAKY!

SPECIAL BRICK
A black chain makes a brilliant finishing touch to a creepy Halloween model.

Round brick as a pillar base

Large, staring eye tiles

Transparent head for a flashing light

Giant vampire bat face over arch

Steps lead to chained-off boarding area

EEK, I WANT MY MUMMY!

🕷

TOP TIP

It's best to use ready-made LEGO roller coaster tracks and car bases. They are made to fit together perfectly.

1x4 curved slope for ear

Curved slope brick

Plate with teeth

Roller coaster car base

Round bricks form pedestal for minifigures

VIEW INSIDE GHOST TRAIN

SPOOKY RIDE

Around the corner it's a beastly sight—gargoyles, skeleton horses, and green-eyed monsters with tentacles. What will you build to give the passengers a scary surprise?

Tail piece makes a good tentacle

Coffin lid with mummy shape

Bat on exit arch gives passengers a final fright

PECULIAR PUMPKINS

Nothing says Halloween quite like a grinning jack-o'-lantern. Make these pleasing pumpkins to display on your windowsill. Or give one away to a friend and bring a smile to their face, too.

Curved bricks form outside edge

Small black radar dish for eye

Green leaf piece

Sloped bricks create holes for eyes

TOP TIP

Build a pumpkin with holes for the eyes and mouth. Then place it in the dark with a flashlight behind it, to light it up!

Plate at the bottom makes a stable stand

MAGIC SPELL CUBE

Have you written any magic spells for Halloween? Build a colorful container to keep your rolled-up spell scrolls together and tidy—and away from snooping eyes!

Write a spell on old paper and roll it up

HEY PRESTO! A SUPER SPELL CUBE!

Tiles on top give a neat finish

BACK VIEW

Bricks with clips hold bone pieces

Glow-in-the-dark spider scares away snoopers

FRONT VIEW

Colored bricks overlap at corners

ROLLIN' TROLL

Make a monstrous motorbike and a tricksy troll to ride it. With this flashy three-wheeler, your biker troll is all set to head out on a Halloween road trip!

WOW... THAT'S A WHEELY COOL BIKE!

Fenders made of curved slopes and windscreens

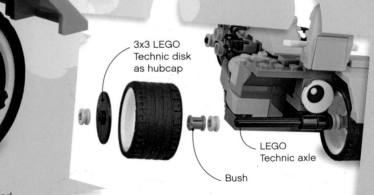

3x3 LEGO Technic disk as hubcap

LEGO Technic axle

Bush

Two broad rear wheels provide stability

REAR WHEEL

SKELETON BAND

These ghoulish giggers look ready to raise a really revolting racket! Build them screeching loudspeakers, a xylobone, and a spooky stage to play on.

HI, FANS! WE'RE THE HALLOWEEN HOWLERS!

Tube-shaped pieces make xylobone's bars

SPECIAL BRICK

1x1 tiles with clips are not just handy for fastening xylobone bars, they are great for accessorizing all your models.

Dome piece creates octopus body

Claws with clips make posable glowing tentacles

1x1 bracket attaches octopus to arch

Two large figure tails create arch

Big cauldron makes a noisy drum

LUCKY NONE OF US HAVE EAR DRUMS!

Horns around the stage protect the band from screaming fans

63

HALLOWEEN TALES

Everybody loves a ghost story! Gather around, pick three LEGO objects from a hat, and make up a spooky story about them. The winner is the most spine-chilling storyteller!

MAGIC POTION

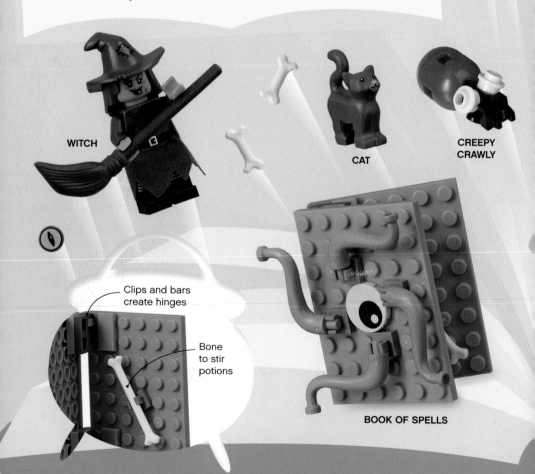

WITCH

CAT

CREEPY CRAWLY

Clips and bars create hinges

Bone to stir potions

BOOK OF SPELLS

HOW TO PLAY

1 Put all the Halloween objects into a hat. You must have at least three times the number of objects as there are players.

2 Taking turns, each player picks three random objects from the hat. Then they tell a story using the three objects.

3 At the end, decide who told the most spellbinding tale of all!

JACK-O'-LANTERN

MUMMY

GARGOYLE

SNAKE

TOP TIP
Find all kinds of Halloween items to go into the hat. Create a mix of creatures, objects, and minifigures. Build some yourself, too!

ZANY ZOMBIES

Zombies are always the life and soul of a Halloween party! Use gray bricks for the heads and arms. Make their legs stiff so they can do a slow zombie shuffle on the dance floor.

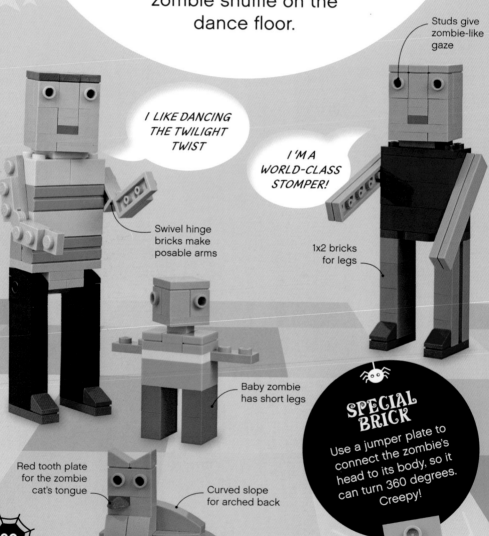

Studs give zombie-like gaze

I LIKE DANCING THE TWILIGHT TWIST

I'M A WORLD-CLASS STOMPER!

Swivel hinge bricks make posable arms

1x2 bricks for legs

Baby zombie has short legs

Red tooth plate for the zombie cat's tongue

Curved slope for arched back

SPECIAL BRICK

Use a jumper plate to connect the zombie's head to its body, so it can turn 360 degrees. Creepy!

CREEPY COFFIN

Make a creepy coffin to lay your minifigures
in for a game of Halloween hide-and-seek.
Build one for your LEGO vampire, too, but don't
be surprised if you hear it creaking open in the night!

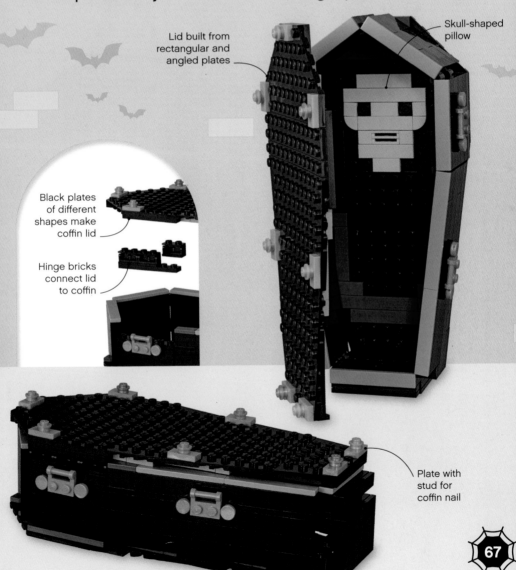

Lid built from
rectangular and
angled plates

Skull-shaped
pillow

Black plates
of different
shapes make
coffin lid

Hinge bricks
connect lid
to coffin

Plate with
stud for
coffin nail

67

Orange plates make
a perfect Halloween-
colored border

Web is attached
to bricks with clips

Black bricks make
a spooky, dark
silhouette

Large, white full-moon
behind house

HAUNTED HOUSE

Build a haunted house that
nobody dares to live in! Make a
dark, looming tower and ramparts
for a ghost to haunt. A guard bat
and a pair of staring eyes will
really warn off intruders.

Black cone
studs form
ramparts

Ghost hangs
on 1x1 brick
with stud

Two 4x2
wedge plates
connected by
plate with hole

*I'M OUT
OF HERE!*

DK
Penguin Random House

SENIOR EDITOR Selina Wood
US EDITOR Megan Douglass
SENIOR DESIGNER Anna Formanek
DESIGNERS James McKeag, Ray Bryant
PRE-PRODUCTION PRODUCER Siu Chan
SENIOR PRODUCER Lloyd Robertson
MANAGING EDITOR Paula Regan
MANAGING ART EDITOR Jo Connor
PUBLISHER Julie Ferris
ART DIRECTOR Lisa Lanzarini
MODEL PHOTOGRAPHY Gary Ombler

MODELS BY Alice Finch, Jason Briscoe
ADDITIONAL MODELS BY Thorin Finch

Dorling Kindersley would like to thank
Randi Sørensen, Heidi K. Jensen, Paul Hansford,
Martin Leighton Lindhardt, Nina Koopmann,
Charlotte Neidhardt, and Torben Vad Nissen at
the LEGO Group; Sadie Smith for proofreading.

First American Edition, 2020
Published in the United States by DK Publishing
1450 Broadway, Suite 801, New York, NY 10018

Page design copyright ©2020
Dorling Kindersley Limited
DK, a Division of Penguin Random House LLC
20 21 22 23 24 10 9 8 7 6 5 4 3 2 1
001–316758–Aug/2020

ISBN 978-0-7440-2151-6

Printed and bound in China

For the curious

www.dk.com
www.LEGO.com

Answers to Spot the Difference on page 17: Panel around shield
piece, door handle, paving stone, grass, spider, gravestone panel,
vine, different-colored tree foliage

MEET THE BUILDERS

ALICE FINCH

Alice travels all around
the world to give talks
about LEGO building.
Alice builds with her
sons, Thorin and
Hadrian, and has built
everything from huge
castles to tiny pet bats.

JASON BRISCOE

Jason's favorite
Halloween model
is the Ghost Ship,
as it reminds him
of pirate stories! He
especially likes the
finger pieces that look
like torn sails.